Flash

CS3

> David Waller

www.payne-gallway.co.uk

✓ Free online support
✓ Useful weblinks
✓ 24 hour online ordering

01865 888070

PAYNE-GALLWAY

Payne-Gallway is an imprint of Pearson Education Limited, a company incorporated in England and Wales, having its registered office at Edinburgh Gate, Harlow, Essex, CM20 2JE. Registered company number: 872828

www.payne-gallway.co.uk

Text © David Waller 2008

First published 2008

12 11 10 09 08
10 9 8 7 6 5 4 3 2 1

British Library Cataloguing in Publication Data
A catalogue record for this book is available from the British Library.

ISBN 978 1 905292 51 6

Designed by Wooden Ark Studios
Edited and typeset by Sparks – www.sparkspublishing.com
Cover design by Wooden Ark Studios
Printed in the UK by Scotprint

Acknowledgements
Every effort has been made to contact copyright holders of material reproduced in this book. Any omissions will be rectified in subsequent printings if notice is given to the publishers.

Original Slurp can design by Frances Sharp

Websites
The websites used in this book were correct and up-to-date at the time of publication. It is essential for tutors to preview each website before using it in class so as to ensure that the URL is still accurate, relevant and appropriate. We suggest that tutors bookmark useful websites and consider enabling students to access them through the school/college intranet.

Ordering Information
Payne-Gallway, FREEPOST (OF1771),
PO Box 381, Oxford OX2 8BR
Tel: 01865 888070
Fax: 01865 314029
Email: orders@payne-gallway.co.uk

CONTENTS

So you know ...

This book is all about using Flash, a program that allows you to animate text and graphics to produce presentations that can be used on websites.

You will first learn some of the skills needed to use Flash and then you will be asked to make decisions about the kinds of animations needed for a particular audience and purpose. This will allow you to show your capability in using ICT and achieve higher National Curriculum levels.

The skills you will learn are:

Task 1: How to draw and animate an object.
Task 2: How to create layers and add buttons and sound.
Task 3: How to add and manipulate graphics, images and text.

You will then be able to use all of the skills you have learnt and the files you have created to carry out the **final project**.

You are eventually going to create an advert for a leisure centre advertising their new café area serving healthy food and drinks. When you have the learned the skills to create everything you'll need, it will be up to you to decide how to use your skills to create the look and feel of your advert.

This screenshot is an example of the features you will be using in Flash and the type of animation you will be creating:

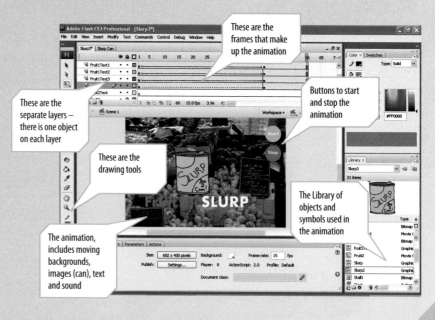

Figure Intro.1

This book also helps you to develop your Functional Skills in ICT. This is all about you being able to use your software skills in the way that best suits the activity that you have been given – in other words, *why* you are doing something in the way that you have chosen. For example, you always need to be thinking about the purpose of what you are doing – what has it got to do with the task, what kind of impact do you want to achieve, who is going to see or use what you're working on (i.e. who is your audience), and what is the background of the situation – for example, do you need to produce a formal or informal document? By considering all of these things you should be able to produce the right kind of documents that are 'fit for purpose', i.e. they do the job they need to do. A lot to take in at once I know, but have a look at the Functional Skills tabs as you work through the book and they'll show you what all this means in practice… so that you can use them to help you with your project.

Before we start with Task 1, though, the next few pages show you some of the most important skills that you'll need throughout your whole project; how to start the program, create new files and save your work. Remember you can return to these pages to remind yourself of these skills if you forget later on in the project.

STARTING THE PROGRAM

Either

Go to **Start** and **All Programs**.

Select the **Adobe** program group and then **Adobe Flash CS3**.

Figure Intro.2

Or

3 Select the Flash shortcut on the desktop.

Figure Intro.3

CREATING A NEW FILE

1 Select **Create New Flash File (ActionScript 2.0)**.

Use ActionScript 2.0 so that it is compatible with Flash 8.

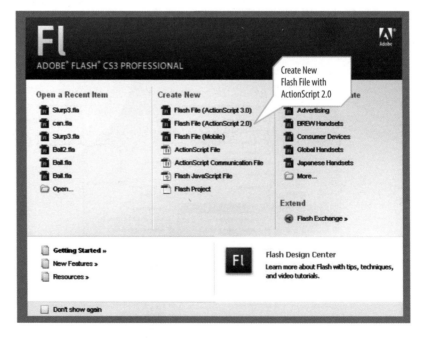

Figure Intro.4

2 You will now see the Flash interface and all of the tools you will need to create an animation. The Stage is the area you will be working in where you create the movies. The call-outs below show you the main features and tools and what they are used for.

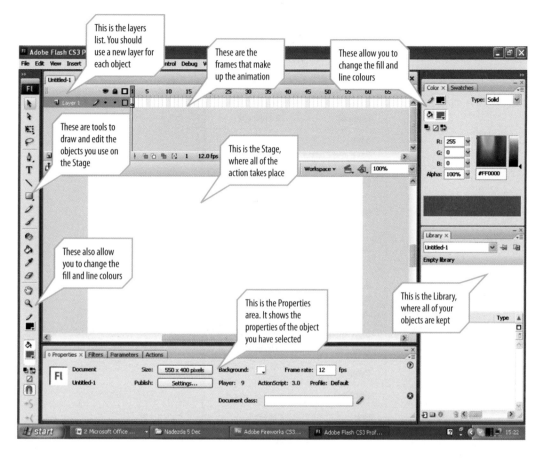

Figure Intro.5

SAVING A FILE

Select **Save As** from the **File** menu.

Figure Intro.6

Now navigate to your home area and save the file in a suitable folder.

You have saved the movie as a Flash project file that you can go back to and edit later on.

It is saved with the extension **.FLA**. So the file below would be **Slurp1.fla**.

Figure Intro.7

PUBLISHING A FILE

When you publish the file, you save it in a format that can be used in a web page or with Flash Player. You *cannot* go back and edit this file.

 Select **Publish** from the **File** menu.

Ⓐ This will publish the file as a Flash (.swf) file.

Adobe Flash CS3 Professional - [Untitled-

| File | Edit | View | Insert | Modify | Text | Commands |

New...	Ctrl+N
Open...	Ctrl+O
Browse...	Ctrl+Alt+O
Open from Site...	
Open Recent	▶
Close	Ctrl+W
Close All	Ctrl+Alt+W
Save	Ctrl+S
Save and Compact	
Save As...	Ctrl+Shift+S
Save as Template...	
Check In...	
Save All	
Revert	
Import	▶
Export	▶
Publish Settings...	Ctrl+Shift+F12
Publish Preview	▶
Publish	Shift+F12
Page Setup...	
Print...	Ctrl+P
Send...	
Edit Sites...	
Exit	Ctrl+Q

Figure Intro.8

The following file would be published:

Slurp1
Flash Movie
4 KB

Figure Intro.9

This is a Flash Movie file and is **Slurp1.swf**.

HOW TO DRAW AND ANIMATE AN OBJECT

TASK BRIEF

The company have sent you an email with the following brief . . .

From: Big Drinks Ltd

To: Design Studio

BRIEF

Slurp is a brand-new, healthy, sugar-free drink aimed at 9–14-year-olds.

We need a digital image of the can, which can be animated as it will be used in online advertisements.

DESIGN STUDIO RESPONSE

 1 The image will be cartoon-like and so a digital photograph cannot be used.

 2 The can will have bright, eye-catching colours.

 3 It will have hand-drawn writing stating the name, 'Slurp', and the slogan, 'Be 2 Cool!'.

4 The can will be animated and move in a circle around the screen while turning through 180°.

As you work through the task you will find out why Design Studio made these choices.

SOFTWARE SKILLS

You will learn how to:

➤ Create a new presentation

➤ Draw and fill an object

➤ Convert the shape into a symbol

➤ Create keyframes

➤ Create motion between the keyframes – tweening

➤ Save the animation

➤ Publish the animation as a Flash file for use on a website

FUNCTIONAL SKILLS

As you work through this task the Functional Skills tabs will explain to you why the design company (Design Studio) responded to the brief from Big Drinks Ltd in the way they did and explain why they would choose to:

➤ Organise documents

➤ Match graphics' style with the audience

➤ Review work

CAPABILITY

You have not been asked to make decisions and design the animation for a particular audience – so you will not be demonstrating **capability**. That will come in later tasks and the project, but you have to learn the basics before you can do that.

VOCABULARY

You should learn some new words and understand what they mean so you can impress people when you next see an animation on television. You'll be able to explain how it was done!

➤ Symbol

➤ Keyframe

➤ Tweening

➤ Publish

RESOURCES

There are two files for this task that demonstrate what you will be creating in Flash:

Slurp1.fla

slurp1.swf

If you want to take a look at these files before you start you can download them from www.payne-gallway.co.uk

⊕ TARGET POINT

Have a look at the statements in this table before you start your task so you know what you are aiming for.

Although you will not be making your own decisions for much of this activity, these levels show you what you could be awarded when completing similar tasks on other work where you are working more independently and without following instructions.

Level 3	Level 4	Level 5	Level 6
You have saved the file with a new name. You saved it as 'Slurp2'.	You have used **Save As** to save the file with a new name – 'Slurp2'.	The image is appropriate for the audience and purpose as listed in the task brief.	The motion of the can is as required in the task brief.
You have saved the file in the correct folder.	You have combined a suitable image and some text – you have drawn the Slurp can and written some text on it.	You have converted the image to a symbol, created key frames and motion between them.	
You have created a file containing some information – you have drawn the Slurp can.	You have positioned and resized the image of the Slurp can.	You have tested the movie to make sure that it runs correctly.	

Now start Flash and let's get started.

Before we get started – a bit of theory.

We are going to use Flash to create movies or animations. Flash creates animations in the same way that they have been created for almost a hundred years: an object is created on one frame and then it is moved slightly on the next frame, and a bit more on the next, etc.

When these frames are viewed quickly in sequence – at say 15 frames per second – it looks as though the object is moving.

That's all there is to it!

OK. Let's get started.

Before you start any project, you should organise your folders where you are going to save the work.

FUNCTIONAL SKILLS

Organising your files and folder structure – we would want to keep our folders organised so that we could easily identify one from another, as we work for several clients and we store our files logically so that we can find them easily at a later date

1 Create a new folder called **Flash**.

2 In the Flash folder, create another folder called **Task1** – this is where you will save the files you will be creating.

STEP 1: CREATING THE SLURP CAN

1 Load **Flash** and create a new **Flash document** – remember to select Flash file (ActionScript 2.0). See page 6.

The Slurp can is going to look cartoon-like and so we do not want lots of straight lines…

FUNCTIONAL SKILLS

Matching the styling tools you use to your need – we have chosen to use a large brush tool, draw the graphic 'freehand' and use bright colours from the palette to a create a cartoon style that will be attractive to a 9–14-year-old audience

Figure 1.1

…but we need some guides to help.

Drawing an oval

2 Select the **Oval Tool**.

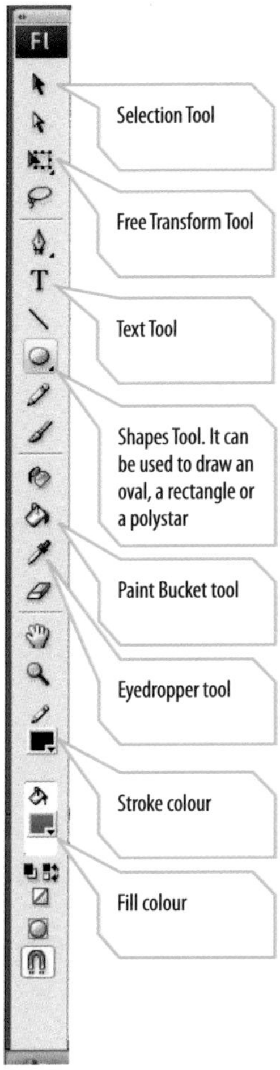

Figure 1.2

It is with all of the other tools at the left of the window.

Selection Tool

Free Transform Tool

Text Tool

Shapes Tool. It can be used to draw an oval, a rectangle or a polystar

Paint Bucket tool

Eyedropper tool

Stroke colour

Fill colour

Figure 1.3

VERY IMPORTANT TIP

If the Shapes Tool is showing a rectangle instead of an oval . . .

Figure 1.4

Point to the arrow at the bottom, right corner and hold down the left mouse button.

*Select the **Oval Tool** from the menu:*

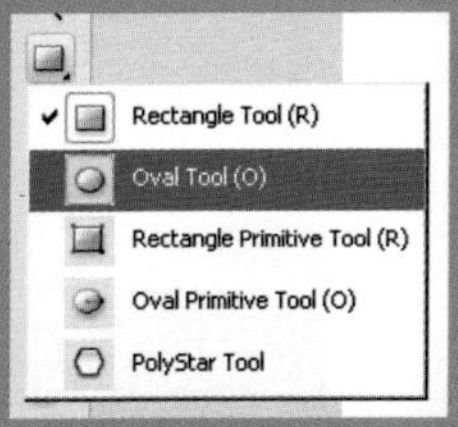

✓	Rectangle Tool (R)
	Oval Tool (O)
	Rectangle Primitive Tool (R)
	Oval Primitive Tool (O)
	PolyStar Tool

Figure 1.5

Setting the stroke colour

3 Set the **stroke colour** to black.

> Click on the **Stroke** icon.

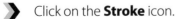

Figure 1.6

> Select the black colour.

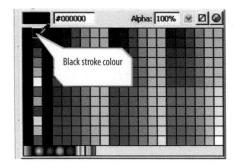

Figure 1.7

Setting the fill colour

 Set the **fill colour** to transparent.

Figure 1.8

> Click on the **Fill** icon.

> Select transparent.

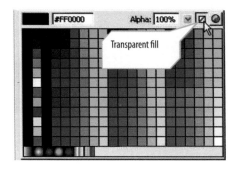

Figure 1.9

5 Draw an oval shape for the top of the can on the Stage.

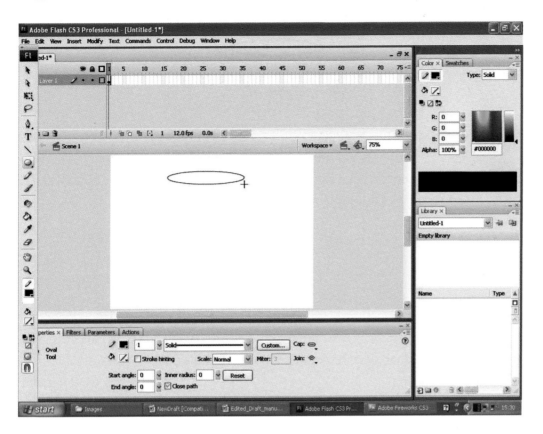

Figure 1.10

IMPORTANT TIPS

Press Ctrl-2 to see all of the Stage.

Press Ctrl and + to zoom in.

Press Ctrl and – to zoom out.

VERY IMPORTANT TIP

When you draw an object you draw a stroke (the line) and a fill.

To select both the stroke and the fill, you should double click the object.

 6 Select the **Selection Tool**.

Figure 1.11

Selecting the stroke and the fill

 7 Double click the oval shape to select both the stroke and the fill.

Figure 1.12

8 Right click on the oval (not on the Stage) and select **Copy**.

9 Right click on the Stage and select **Paste** to paste the copy for the bottom of the can.

Figure 1.13

 10 Now select and drag the copy to its position for the bottom of the can.

When the copy is almost directly under the top of the can, a guide line will appear.

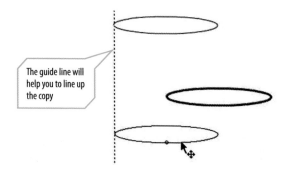

The guide line will help you to line up the copy

Figure 1.14

Now that the top and bottom are in place, we have to draw the sides of the can.

Drawing straight lines

 11 Select the **Line Tool**.

Figure 1.15

12 Draw lines for the sides of the can.

Figure 1.16   *Figure 1.17*

IMPORTANT TIP

When you are using the Line Tool, if you hold down the Shift key the line will be perfectly straight.

This drawing is going to act as a guide for the Slurp can. The actual can is going to be drawn on a new layer.

Inserting a layer

13 Click on the **Insert layer** icon ...

Figure 1.18

... and a new layer is created. The blue colour shows it is now the active layer.

Figure 1.19

The can is now going to be drawn on this layer (Layer 2) using the **Brush Tool**. Layer 2 is over Layer 1 and so the shapes on Layer 1 can be used as guides.

Using the Brush Tool

14 Select the **Brush Tool**.

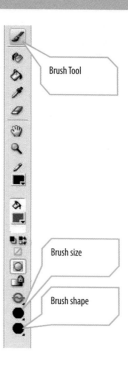

Brush Tool

Figure 1.20

When you select the Brush Tool, the new icons shown in Figure 1.21 will appear at the bottom of the tools bar.

15 Click on the **Brush size** icon and select the third size.

Brush size

Brush shape

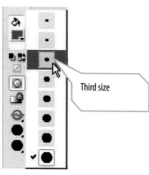

Third size

Figure 1.21

Figure 1.22

16 Now use the brush to draw the outline of the can and the ring-pull as shown in Figure 1.23.

IMPORTANT TIP

If you make a mistake, you can cancel the last actions by pressing Ctrl-z.

Figure 1.23

Using the Paint Bucket Tool

17 Select the **Paint Bucket Tool** to fill areas of the can.

Figure 1.24

18 Set the **Fill** colour for the different areas.

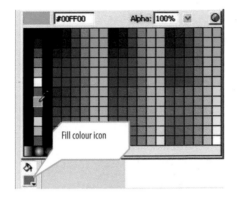

Figure 1.25

19 Fill the areas of the can – remember you can zoom in and out using Ctrl and + and Ctrl and -.

Figure 1.26

When you are filling the ring-pull, you will have to draw a line to stop the fill spilling over onto the can lid.

Figure 1.27

20 Use the Brush Tool to add the writing as shown in Figure 1.28.

Figure 1.28

Deleting a layer

21 Now **delete** Layer 1 by selecting Layer 1 and clicking on the delete layer icon.

This layer had the guide on it and we don't need it any more.

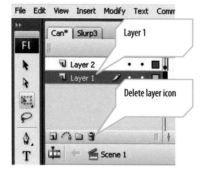

Figure 1.29

Renaming a layer

22 Double click on the Layer 2 name and rename it as Slurp Can.

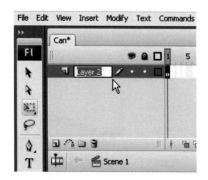

Figure 1.30

Congratulations! You now have a completed can. It is very important that you keep this in case you have problems later on. So save this Flash file as **Slurp**.

If you mess up later work you can always load this one again so you don't have to start from the beginning!

STEP 2: ANIMATING THE SLURP CAN

Now that we have created the can, we can use it to create a simple animation.

We are going to make the can move around the screen in a circle and twist it through 180° as it does so.

Figure 1.31

Figure 1.34

Figure 1.33

OK. Let's get started!

  Open the **Slurp** file and use **Save As** to save it with a new name.

Call it **Slurp1**.

  Select the **Selection Tool** and draw round the can to select all of the separate parts.

Figure 1.35   *Figure 1.36*   *Figure 1.37*

Converting to a symbol

3 We can now convert the can into a **symbol**.

Either

Select **Modify > Convert to Symbol**:

Figure 1.38

Or

Press **F8**.

4 Name the symbol as **Slurp** and make it a **Graphic** symbol.

Figure 1.39

The new symbol will appear in the **Symbol Library**.

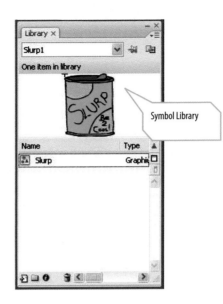

Figure 1.40

We are going to animate the can by changing its position on each frame and then run through the frames very quickly so it looks as though the can is moving. We are going to use 60 frames. That may seem a lot of work to do but don't worry – Flash is clever and can do most of the work for us.

All we have to do is create a few **keyframes** and let Flash create the ones in between.

This is called **Creating Motion Tween**.

Changing the frame rate

  We must, firstly, set the **Frame Rate** by double clicking on the frame rate shown.

The **Document Properties** box will appear.

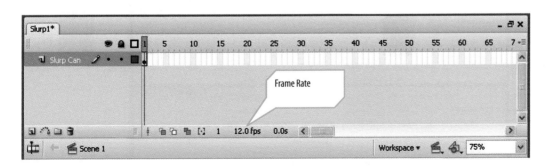

Figure 1.41

6 Set the frame rate to 15 frames per second (fps) and click on **OK**.

Figure 1.42

At the moment there is only one frame.

7 Position the can at the bottom left-hand side of frame 1 – this is where the can will start from and this is also where we want the can to finish at the end of the animation.

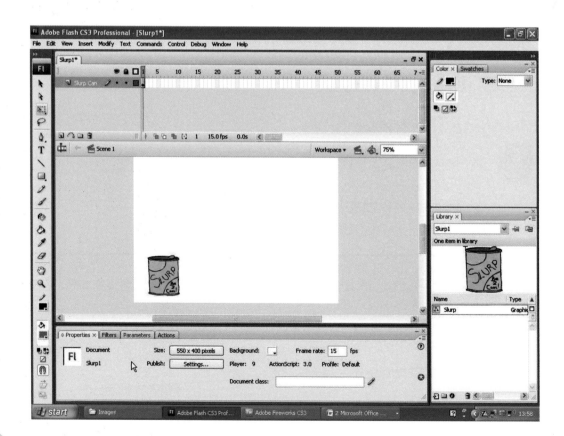

Figure 1.43

The animation will last for four seconds – that is, 60 frames. (Remember, we set the frame rate per second as 15.) So we want the can in exactly this position on frame 60.

Creating keyframes

 Right click on frame 60 of the Slurp can layer and select **Insert Keyframe**.

Figure 1.44

A keyframe is inserted at frame 60. It contains the can in the same position as it was on frame 1.

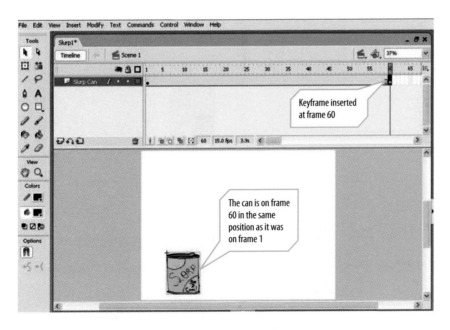

Figure 1.45

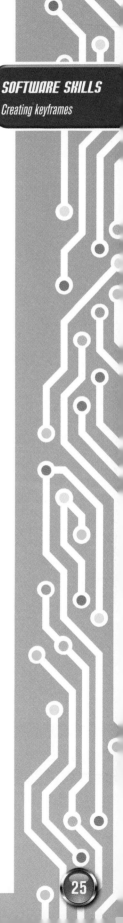

9 Insert a keyframe at frame 15 – that is the one-second mark.

Figure 1.46

… Frame 15 is now selected.

10 Move the can where it should be at frame 15 (you might like to use the guides to help you do this).

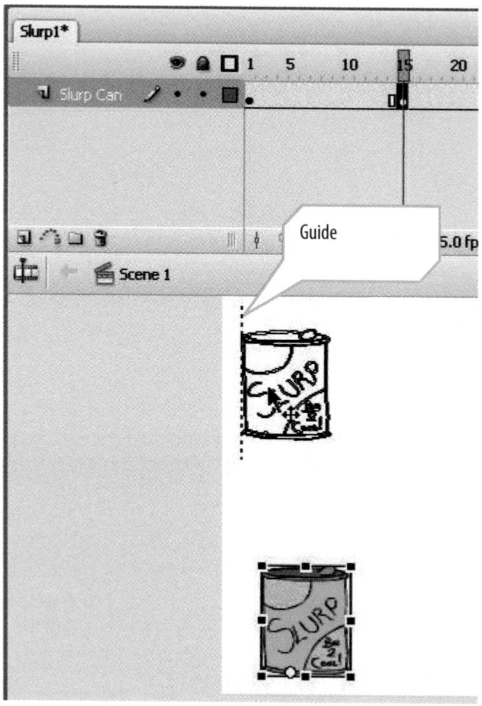

Figure 1.47

Using the Free Transform Tool

11 Now we have to rotate the can by selecting the **Free Transform Tool**.

Figure 1.48

12 Move the mouse pointer to the top, right corner of the can so that it turns into the **rotate pointer**…

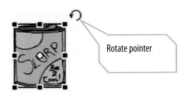

Rotate pointer

Figure 1.49

13 Now drag the mouse to rotate the can through 90°.

Figure 1.50

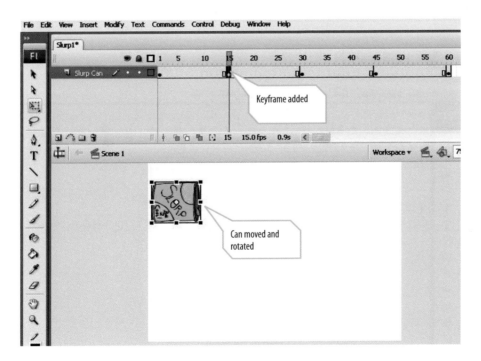

Keyframe added

Can moved and rotated

Figure 1.51

This process must now be repeated at frames **30** and **45**.

》 Frame 30

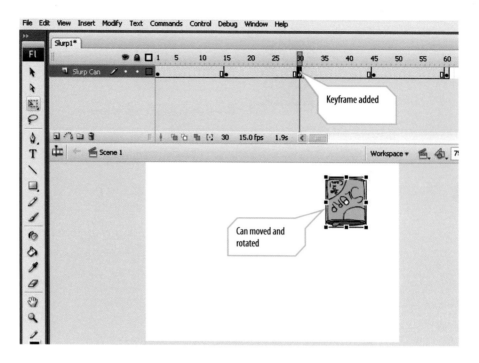

Figure 1.52

》 Frame 45

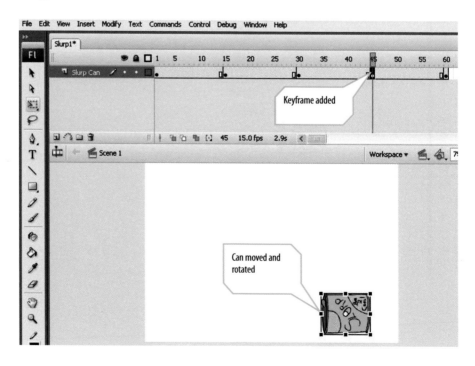

Figure 1.53

Creating Motion Tween

15   Now for the 'tween' to create the animation.

Right click on a frame between frame 1 and frame 15 and select **Create Motion Tween**.

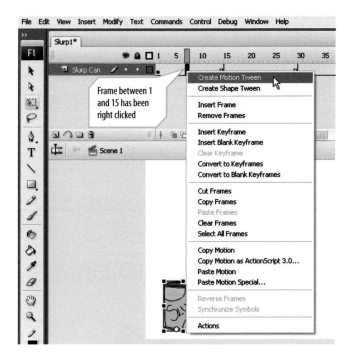

Figure 1.54

The arrow between frames 1 and 15 shows that motion has been created.

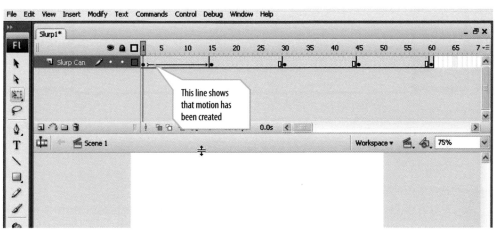

Figure 1.55

16 Now we must do the same between all of the keyframes – between frames 15 and 30, frames 30 and 45, and frames 45 and 60.

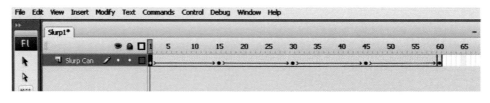

Figure 1.56

17 Congratulations! The animation is complete. Don't forget to save it again!

Testing the movie

SOFTWARE SKILLS

Testing the movie

To test that it works press Ctrl-Enter. A window will open running your animation.

FUNCTIONAL SKILLS

Reviewing your work – we would always test our work before sending it to a client so that we remove any mistakes before they see it, as this would make a bad impression

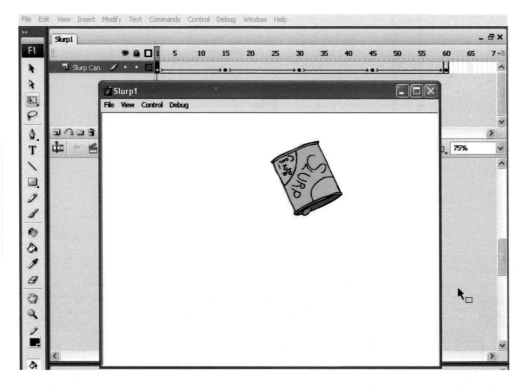

Figure 1.57

Magic!

18 Close this window in the normal way by clicking on the red cross at the top right corner.

19 Now **Publish** the file. Publish it in the Flash folder as **Flash1** (See page 9 if you can't remember how to do this).

ALL DONE

That's it! Task 1 is now complete.

CHECKPOINT

Check that you know how to:

❯ Draw an object.

❯ Select an object.

❯ Apply colour fills and strokes to an object.

❯ Add, delete or rename a layer.

❯ Use the Brush tool and the Paint Bucket Tool.

❯ Move and rotate an object.

❯ Convert an object to a symbol.

❯ Change the frame rate.

❯ Create keyframes.

❯ Use the Free Transform Tool.

❯ Create a motion tween.

❯ Save your file.

❯ Test and publish your movie.

ASSESSMENT POINT

Now let's assess the work. Look back at the table at the beginning of this section (**Target point**) and decide on which of the statements you can answer 'Yes' to.

Did you do as well as you expected? Could you improve your work? Add a comment to your work to show what you could do to improve it so that next time you'll remember to do it the first time.

TASK BRIEF

They loved your can and its animation, and have selected you to create the online advert. They have sent you a new email ...

From: Big Drinks Ltd

To: Design Studio

BRIEF

The can design and the animation are just what we are looking for, as it presents the right image to the age group we are targeting. We would now like you to use the animation as part of an advert that we can use on our website.

DESIGN STUDIO RESPONSE

 1   The word 'Slurp' and the phrase 'Be 2 Cool!' will be able to move in different ways around the screen.

 2   There will be two buttons for a user to click to start the text moving.

3   When the text moves there will be different sounds playing.

As you work through the task you will find out why Design Studio made these choices.

SOFTWARE SKILLS

You will use the skills from Task 1 and learn these new skills:

> **Add** more layers
> **Rename** layers
> **Drawing skills** for different objects
> Add and program **command buttons** to allow the users to move different objects
> Add an **audio soundtrack**

FUNCTIONAL SKILLS

As you work through this task the Functional Skills tabs will explain to you why the design company (Design Studio) responded to the brief from Big Drinks Ltd in the way they did and explain why they would choose to:

> Combine different types of files
> Animate objects
> Make the advert interactive

CAPABILITY

You will show that you can:

> Write a sequence of events to control movement on the screen

> Test your animation to check that it works correctly

VOCABULARY

You should learn some new words and understand what they mean.

> Timeline
> Timeline label
> Command button

RESOURCES

There are two files for this task that demonstrate what you will be creating in Flash:

Slurp2.fla

slurp2.swf

If you want to take a look at these files before you start you can download them from www.payne-gallway.co.uk

Level 3	Level 4	Level 5	Level 6
You have saved the file with a new name. You saved it as 'Slurp2'.	You have used **Save As** to save the file with a new name – 'Slurp2'.	You have combined an image with text and sound – you have drawn the Slurp can and added sound and text on the buttons.	You have added buttons and written the instructions to make them play the animation.
You have saved the file in the correct folder.	You have combined a suitable image and some text – you have drawn the Slurp can and some text on the buttons.	You have put stop commands on to the timeline to stop the animation.	You have completed an interactive presentation so that the user can control the animation.
You have created a file containing some information – you have drawn the Slurp can.	You have positioned and resized the image of the Slurp can.	You have tested the buttons to ensure that they work.	You have checked that all of the code has been entered correctly.
You have presented information for a particular purpose – you have created a Slurp can to advertise the drink.			

 **TARGET POINT**

Have a look at the statements in this table before you start your task so you know what you are aiming for.

Although you will not be making your own decisions for much of this activity, these levels show you what you could be awarded when completing similar tasks on other work where you are working more independently and without following instructions.

Before we get started, there are two main rules to remember when using Flash:

1 All objects must be converted to symbols.

2 Every symbol you want to move independently should be on its own layer.

OK. Let's get started.

Before you start any project, you should organise your area where you are going to save the work.

In the Flash folder, create another folder called **Task2** – this is where you will save the files you will be creating in this project.

In this task we are going to make the text on the can move when a command button is pressed. This allows the user to interact with the animation. The text is going to move around a set path.

The finished animation will look like this on the Stage:

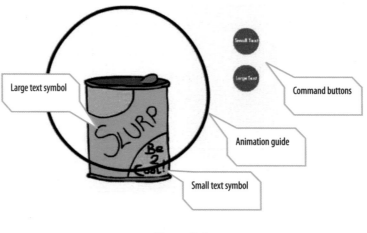

Figure 2.1

This is a far more complicated animation and will need nine layers:

Figure 2.2

PREPARATION

Before we start we need to gather our resources or assets.

 1 Load the original **Slurp** file and save it as **Slurp2**.

 2 Set the frame rate to 15 frames per second (see pages 23–24).

 3 In this animation we are going to use two sound files that should each last for four seconds. You can cut and edit audio files in a program like Audacity. In this example the audio files are called NewAgeTechno and SaxyGroovy.

OK, that's everything. So let's get started.

STEP 1: CREATING THE SYMBOLS

 1 The can should look like this on the Stage. There should be one layer called **Slurp Can**.

Figure 2.3

If it is too large, then:

> Select the **Selection Tool** (Figure 2.4)

> Draw a frame around the can to select all of the elements.

> Use the **Free Transform Tool** to resize the can (Figure 2.5). (Hold down the Shift key and use a resize box at a corner of the object.)

Figure 2.4 *Figure 2.5*

You have used these tools before, in Task 1.

2 The writing on the can must be turned into **symbols** so that it can be animated.

❯ Use the Selection Tool and hold down the Shift key to select all of the letters in the word 'Slurp'.

All letters in the word 'Slurp' selected

Figure 2.6

❯ Now convert it into a symbol called **LargeText** by clicking **Modify > Convert to Symbol** or by pressing **F8**.

❯ Save the 'Slurp' letters as a Graphic symbol called LargeText.

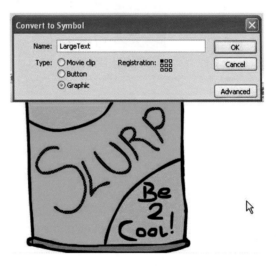

Figure 2.7

3 Now do the same for the 'Be 2 Cool!' letters and call the graphic symbol, **SmallText**.

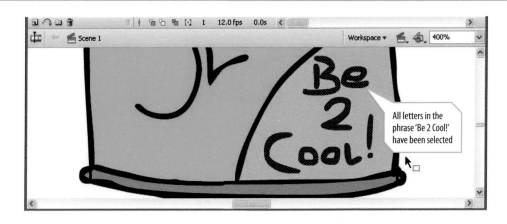

Figure 2.8

4 When we move these symbols, we have a problem. There is no background colour where the symbol used to be!

Figure 2.9

This can be easily rectified.

Using the Eyedropper Tool

5 Select the **Eyedropper Tool**.

Figure 2.10

6 Click in the green area to set the fill colour to the correct shade of green.

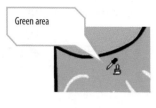

Figure 2.11

7 Now use the **Paint Bucket Tool** and click on the white areas left by the letters to fill in the areas and leave them green.

Figure 2.12

8 Do the same for the SmallText (Be 2 Cool!) and then move the symbols back into place on the can so it looks like Figure 2.13.

Figure 2.13

As each piece of text is going to move independently, they should be on separate layers.

9 Select the LargeText symbol and press the Delete key.

Figure 2.14

Figure 2.15

Don't worry! It's still in the Library.

Figure 2.16

10

Now do the same for SmallText. The Stage should now look like this:

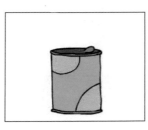

Figure 2.17

Creating a new layer

11

We now have to create new layers for LargeText and SmallText. Click the **New layer** icon, to create a new layer.

Figure 2.18

Renaming a layer

 12 Double click the layer and rename it as LargeText. Keep it selected.

Figure 2.19

 13 **Make sure the new layer is selected** and move in the LargeText symbol from the Library by clicking on it and, while holding the left-hand mouse button down, dragging the symbol onto the Stage and positioning it in its correct place on the can. See Figure 2.20.

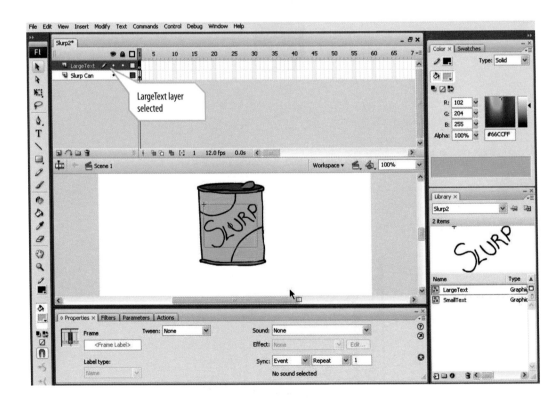

Figure 2.20

14 Now repeat this process for the **SmallText** symbol.

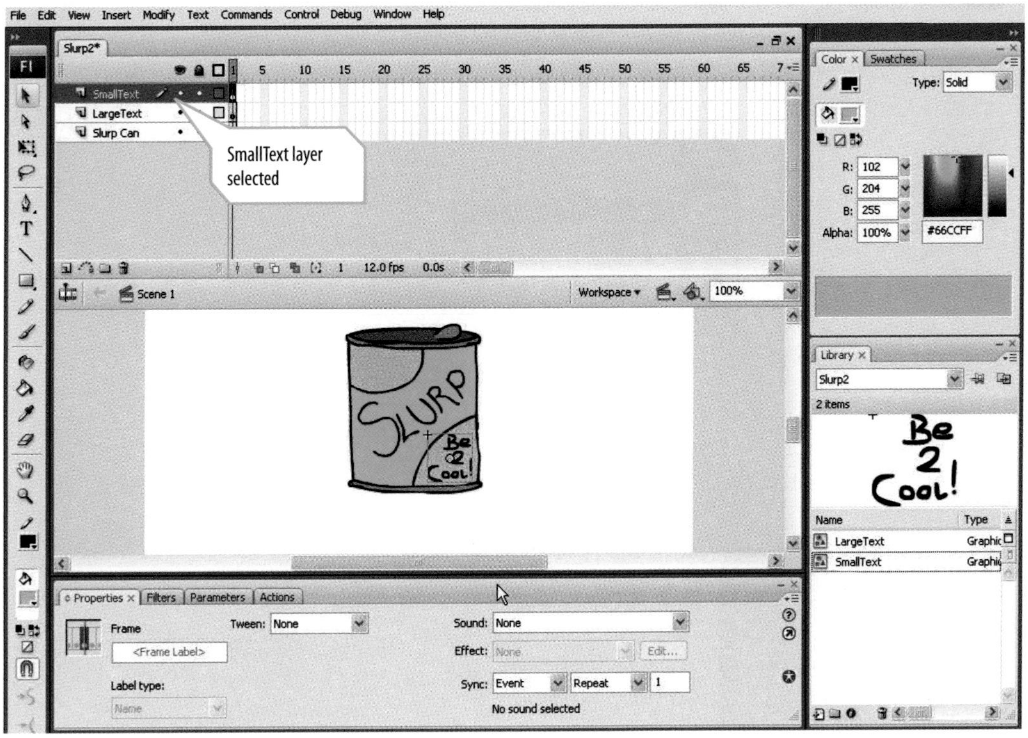

Figure 2.21

STEP 2: ANIMATING THE SMALLTEXT SYMBOL

The SmallText symbol is going to move around a **Motion Guide**.

A motion guide must be placed in its own layer and be immediately above the layer it is controlling.

1 Make sure the SmallText layer is highlighted and create a new layer.

It will be created immediately above the highlighted layer but even if it wasn't we can drag layers up and down the list.

Creating a motion guide

 2 Rename this new layer as **Guide** by double clicking on it and typing in the new name.

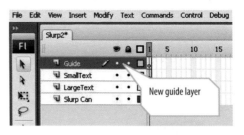

Figure 2.22

 3 Make sure the Guide layer is highlighted and use the **Oval Tool** to draw a circle.

IMPORTANT TIP
You can use the **Oval Tool** to draw a circle if you press the Shift key while drawing.

Figure 2.23

 4 Give it a black outline and no fill. Also, make sure that it passes over the **SmallText** symbol – as shown in Figure 2.24.

Figure 2.24

We now have to convert this layer to a guide.

 5 Right click the layer and select **Guide** from the menu.

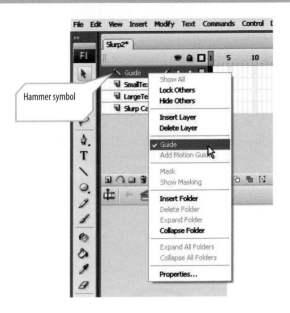

Figure 2.25

It will now have a hammer symbol on it telling you that Flash knows it is a Motion Guide.

Now we can animate the SmallText symbol using the circle in the Guide layer as a guide.

 Select the SmallText layer.

We want the movement of the symbol to take four seconds – therefore, right click frame 60 on this layer and insert a keyframe.

This means that the text will finish where it started.

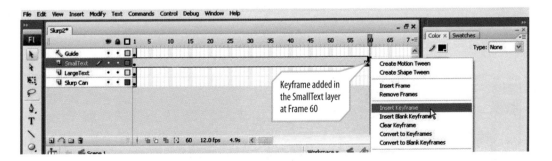

Figure 2.26

If you click on Frame 60 of the SmallText layer, all you can see is the symbol we called SmallText.

We cannot see the guide or the can!

Therefore, right click on frame 60 of the **Guide layer** and select **Insert Frame** – not a keyframe.

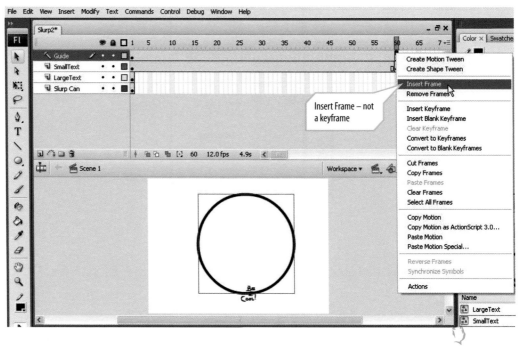

Figure 2.27

Now we can see the guide on all 60 frames.

We want the text not only to follow the guide but also to spin round through 360° so we will need to use the **Free Transform Tool** again. Let's see how we do it.

 Make a keyframe on **frame 10** of the **SmallText** layer by right clicking it and selecting **Insert Keyframe**.

Figure 2.28

Now use the **Selection Tool** to drag the SmallText symbol along the guide, as shown in Figure 2.29.

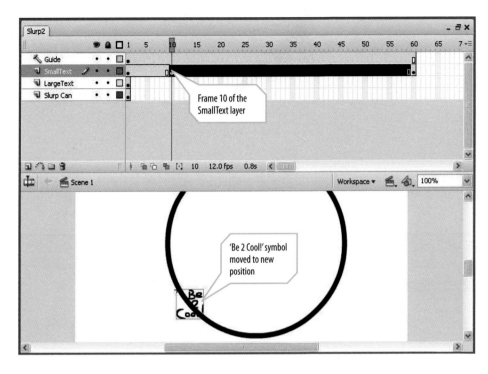

Figure 2.29

Rotating a symbol

 Select the **Free Transform Tool** and rotate and move the pointer near the corner of the SmallText symbol until it changes to the rotate shape, as shown in Figure 2.30.

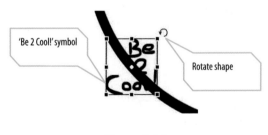

Figure 2.30

11 Now rotate the symbol clockwise through about 60°, as shown in Figure 2.31.

SmallText symbol rotated clockwise through about 60°

Figure 2.31

12 Insert another keyframe at frame 20. Move the text symbol along the motion guide and rotate it a bit more in the same direction as before, as shown in Figure 2.32.

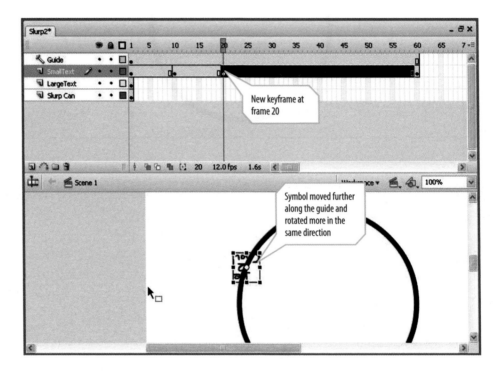

New keyframe at frame 20

Symbol moved further along the guide and rotated more in the same direction

Figure 2.32

13 Do the same for frames 30, 40 and 50 until the text symbol is almost back where it started on your motion guide. Remember that at frame 60, it is back where it started.

Keyframes added at frames 10, 20, 30, 40 and 50

Figure 2.33

14

Now we have to right click between each of the keyframes and click on **Create Motion Tween**.

There should now be arrows linking the keyframes on the SmallText layer.

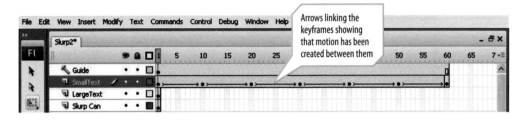

Figure 2.34

We nearly forgot about the Slurp can – it's only showing on frame 1.

Inserting frames

15

Select the Slurp Can layer and by right clicking on frame 60 **Insert Frame** at frame 60.

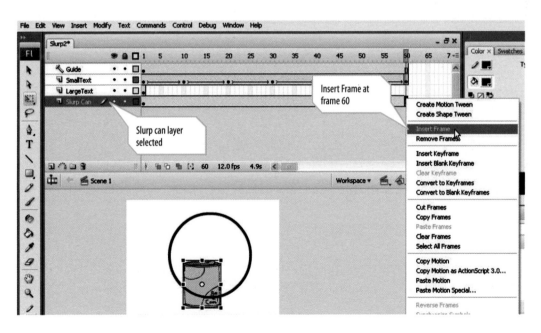

Figure 2.35

The Slurp can will now be on all the frames between 1 and 60.

OK, time for a demonstration. Save the file (**Slurp2**) and press Ctrl-Enter to run it.

You should see the text symbol circling around the can without the guide, as in Figure 2.36.

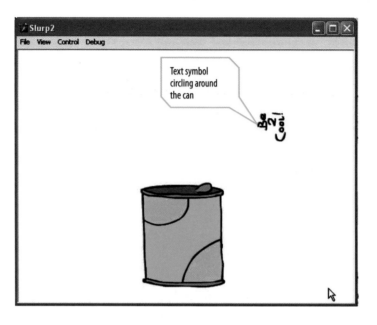

Figure 2.36

Congratulations!

STEP 3: ADDING SOUND FOR THE SMALLTEXT ANIMATION

Now we are going to add some music that will play while the SmallText symbol is moving. You will need an audio file and you should edit it to last four seconds – that is, 60 frames. You can use free software such as Audacity to do this.

Importing sound

 Go to the **File** menu and select **Import > Import to Library**.

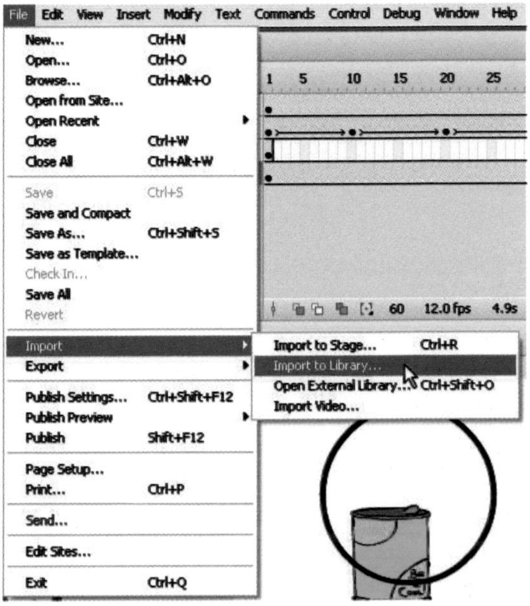

Figure 2.37

 Navigate to your sound file and select it. You should see it appear in the Library.

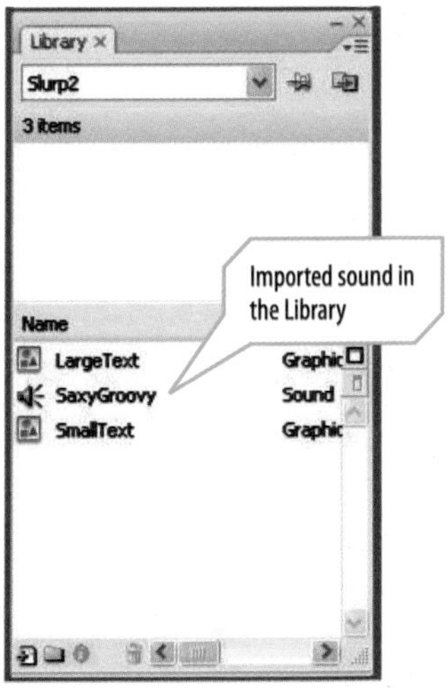

Figure 2.38

FUNCTIONAL SKILLS

Combining file types – as the advert is online we can use both sound and graphics, and this will help to make the advert more memorable to the audience

SOFTWARE SKILLS

Importing sound

3 Create a new **layer** and rename it as **Sound 1**.

Drag it so that it is just underneath the **SmallText** layer.

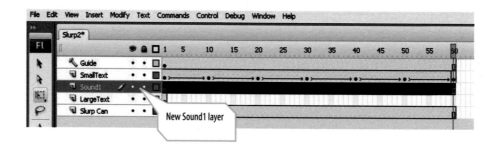

Figure 2.39

4 Click on frame 1 of this layer and drag the sound from the Library to the Stage.

You will see it appear on the timeline.

Figure 2.40

To finish off this section, we need to show the LargeText symbol between frames 1 and 60.

So right click on frame 60 of the LargeText layer and **Insert frame**.

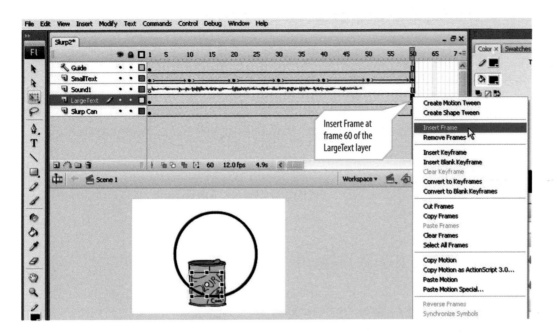

Figure 2.41

Go on, let's try it out again. Press Ctrl-Enter.

Brilliant!

STEP 4: ANIMATING THE LARGETEXT SYMBOL AND ADDING SOUND

Now we've got to animate the LargeText symbol.

We need to animate this one between frames 60 and 120.

But before we start, let's get the other layers ready, as we need the Slurp can and the SmallText symbol to stay where they are between frames 60 and 120 when the LargeText symbol is moving.

 Right click on frame 120 of the **Slurp Can** and **SmallText** layers and select **Insert Frame**.

Now these will still be visible while we animate the LargeText symbol.

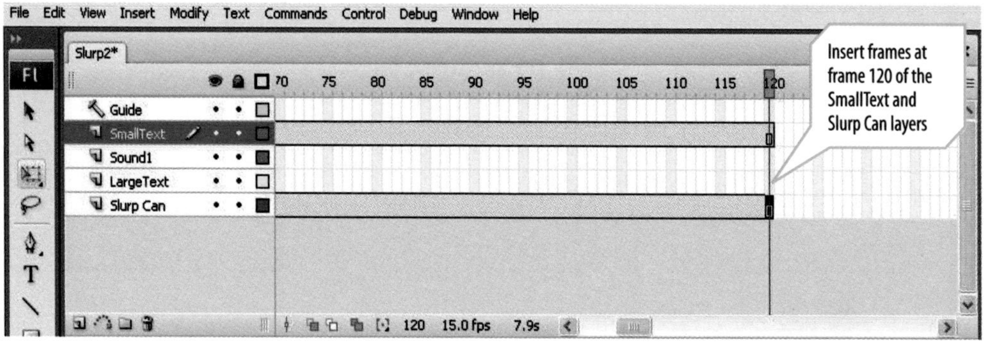

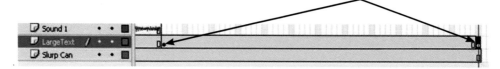

Figure 2.42

 Right click on frame 61 of the **LargeText** layer and **Insert Keyframe**.

Do the same on frame 120 to insert another keyframe.

We can now animate the LargeText symbol between these keyframes.

Figure 2.43

This time we are going to move the text up to the top left corner of the screen and then move it back again. As it moves up to the top left it is going to get smaller and then get bigger as it moves back.

Insert a keyframe at frame 75 of the LargeText layer – this is one second after frame 60 as we set the frame rate to 15 frames per second.

➤ At frame 75 use the **Selection Tool** to move the **LargeText** symbol up to the top left of the Stage.

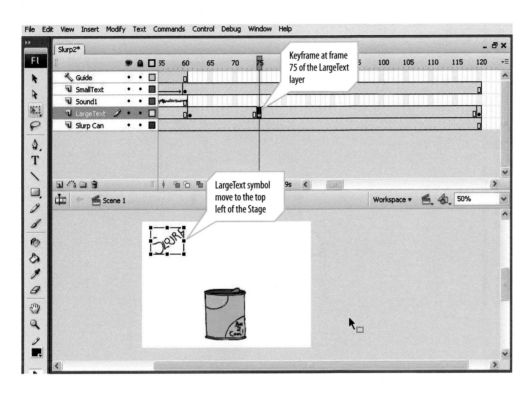

Figure 2.44

➤ Use the **Free Transform Tool** to make it smaller.

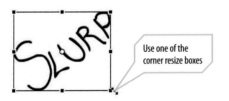

Use one of the corner resize boxes

IMPORTANT TIP

If you hold down the Shift key and use one of the corner resize boxes, the symbol proportions will say the same.

Figure 2.45

Now insert a keyframe at frame 90.

Move the text back to the can and enlarge it using the **Free Transform Tool**.

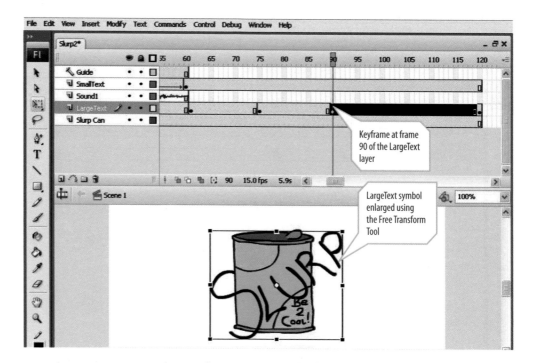

Figure 2.46

 Insert a keyframe in the LargeText layer at frame 105.

Don't change the LargeText symbol as we want it to remain large for one second.

 Frame 120 has already been created so now right click between the keyframes on the LargeText layer and **Create Motion Tween** them.

Figure 2.47

 Now we need to add some sound for this animation.

Go to **File** > **Import** > **Import to Stage** as you did for the other sound file.

Select your sound file and click on **Open**.

You should now see the sound file in the Library.

Create a new layer and rename it as **Sound 2**.

Drag it so that it is underneath the LargeText layer.

Figure 2.48

 Insert a **keyframe** at frame 61 of the Sound 2 layer.

Make sure that frame 61 of the Sound2 layer is still selected and drag the new sound from the Library to the Stage.

This will insert the sound from frames 61 to 120 – the same frames that the LargeText animation runs in.

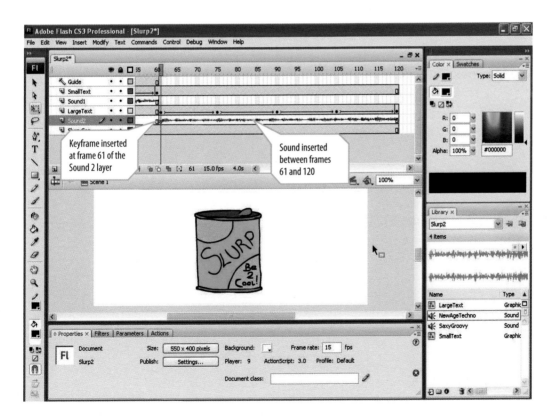

Figure 2.49

Go on! Try it again. Press Ctrl-Enter. Each animation should play in turn with its own sound.

STEP 5: CREATING BUTTONS TO CONTROL THE MOVIE

At the moment, the SmallText moves and then the LargeTest moves, each with its own sound.

We are now going to do some more advanced work that will make the animation interactive.

We are going to add a control layer that will start and stop the animation at fixed points and then add buttons to allow the user to control it.

 Create a new layer and rename it as **Control** and move it to the top of the layers.

Figure 2.50

We want to **stop** the animation from running until a user pushes a button.

So we want to stop the animation at frame 1.

Adding an action to a frame

 Click in **frame 1** of the **Control layer**.

Now click on the **Actions** tab, which you will find under the Stage – we are going to create an action for this frame.

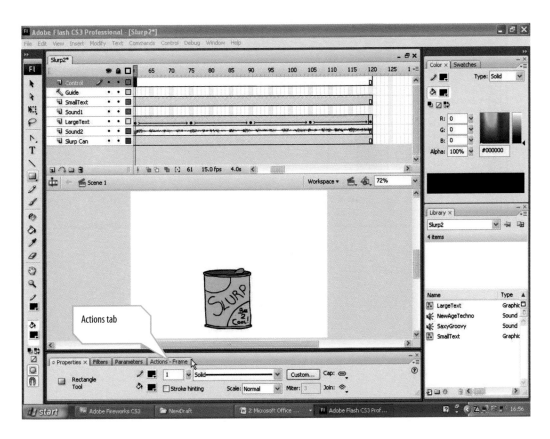

Figure 2.51

VERY IMPORTANT TIP

If the Actions tab is not there, select Actions from the Window menu. Minimise it when you have finished.

The Actions pane will now open.

We now have to write a bit of **Action Script** or code to say what the action is going to be.

When writing code we have to be very, very careful. It must be written exactly right or Flash will not be able to understand it.

So in the Actions pane write the following – exactly as it appears here:

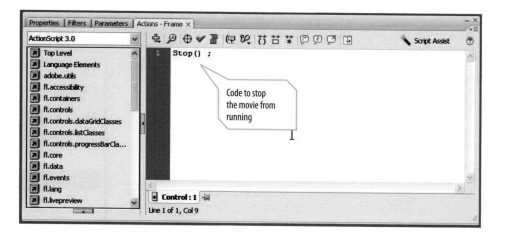

Figure 2.52

That's:

```
Stop() ;
```

This tells Flash to stop at this frame before it runs the SmallText animation.

 Minimise the Actions frame and click on the Properties tab so you can see the properties of the objects.

OK. So how are we going to get Flash to start running the animation?

We will have to tell it to go to another frame and start running.

That means we will have to give the frame a label, so we can tell Flash where to go.

Labelling a frame

5 Right click in **frame 2** of the Control layer and insert a keyframe.

Left click on frame 2 of the Control layer and give the frame a label.

Figure 2.53

We are going to tell Flash to go to the SmallText frame and start running.

We are going to have to tell it to stop again at frame 60 where the SmallText animation finishes.

6 Right click in frame **60** of the Control layer and insert a keyframe.

Left click in this keyframe and type in the following code in the Actions pane:

```
Stop() ;
```

Figure 2.54

We now have to give frame 61 a label.

What shall we call it? Yes, that's right – we'll call it LargeText.

Right click in frame 61 and insert a keyframe.

So left click in frame **61** and give it the label, LargeText.

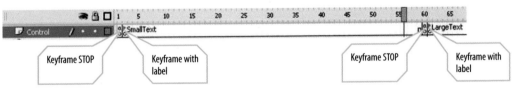

Figure 2.55

The Control frame should now look like this:

Figure 2.56

We have now set up the controls and labelled the frames.

All we have to do is create two buttons that tell Flash which of the two labels to go to – either the SmallText label or the LargeText label.

Create a new layer and rename it as **Button1**.

This layer could be anywhere in the stack, but to make it easier to see, drag it to the bottom.

Figure 2.57

 Make sure that frame 1 of this layer is selected as we are now going to create the button.

If you are good at computer graphics, you can make the button very flashy, but a basic one works just as well.

Select the **Oval Tool** and give it a red stroke and a red fill.

Now, holding down the Shift key, draw a circle on the layer – as shown in Figure 2.58.

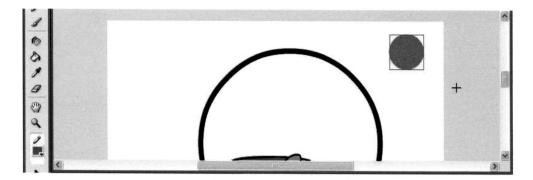

Figure 2.58

Adding text

 12 Make sure the circle object is deselected and now select the **Text Tool** T .

Change both the stroke and fill to white.

You can change the font and font size by using the Properties pane at the bottom of the screen.

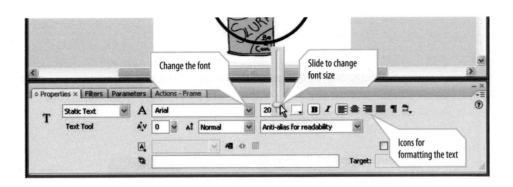

Figure 2.59

 13 Left click over the red button and type **Small Text**.

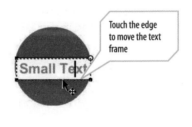

Figure 2.60

You can highlight the text as you would in a word processor and change the size and font.

You can also resize and move the frame.

When you are satisfied, click outside the text to deselect it.

We now have to convert the circle and text into a symbol.

IMPORTANT TIP

If you want to move a selected object by very small amounts, select it using the Selection Tool and use the cursor keys.

Creating a button symbol

 14 Select the **Selection Tool** and draw round the button to select both the circle and the text.

Figure 2.61

15 Now press **F8** to convert it into a symbol or go to **Modify > Convert to Symbol**.

Set the symbol type to **Button**.

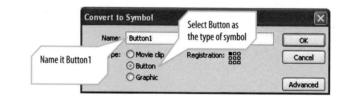

Figure 2.62

16 We now have to create another button in the same way.

Create a new layer under the Button 1 layer and rename it as **Button2**.

On this new layer create a circle and text and convert them into a **symbol** called **Button2**.

Figure 2.63

Now all we have to do is to add some Action script to the buttons.

Button1 will tell Flash to go to the SmallText label and play the animation.

Button2 will tell Flash to go to the LargeText label and play the animation.

Adding actions to a button

 17 Select the Button1 layer containing the Small Text button – this will select the button.

Open the Actions pane.

Type in the following commands – it must be exact!

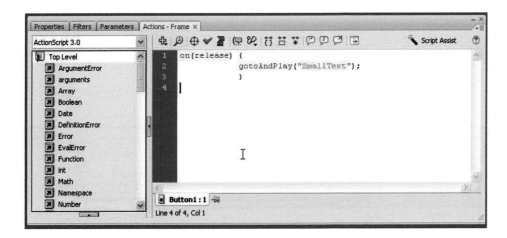

Figure 2.64

That is:

```
on(release) {
gotoAndPlay('SmallText');
}
```

This tells Flash to go to the SmallText label and start playing when a user releases the button.

It will play until it hits the Stop command at frame 60.

 18 Now all we have to do is to add the code for the Button2 symbol.

It's just the same, except it commands Flash to go to the LargeText label.

Select the Button2 layer, open the Actions pane and enter the following code:

```
on(release) {
gotoAndPlay('LargeText');
}
```

Go on. Try it out.

Works pretty well, but there is a problem! The first music plays before anything is pressed!

Solving problems and correcting mistakes is an important part of creating any animation.

In this case, it looks as though we should start Sound 1 on frame 2 rather than frame 1.

Removing frames

19 Highlight the whole of the timeline of the **Sound1** layer. Right click and go to **Remove Frames**.

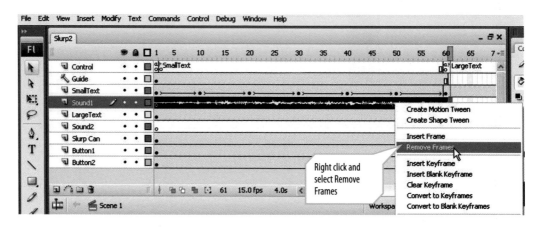

Figure 2.65

20 Right click in **frame 2** of the Sound 1 layer and insert a keyframe.

Drag the sound file from the Library to the Stage.

Insert a keyframe at frame 60.

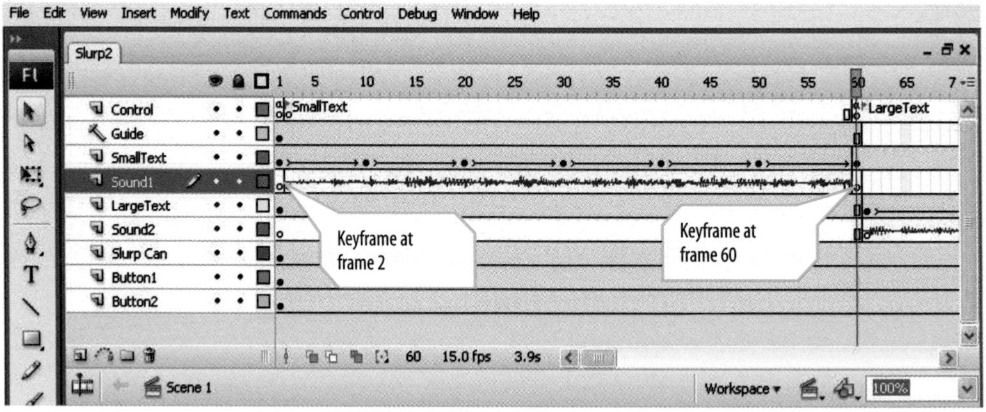

Figure 2.66

ALL DONE

Try it again. It works perfectly. You have debugged it well!

Don't forget to save it and also publish it, so that it can be viewed by people who do not have the Flash program.

CHECKPOINT

You should be able to:

➤ Load a Flash file and save it with a new name.

➤ Use the Eyedropper Tool

➤ Add and rename new layers.

➤ Convert objects to graphic symbols.

➤ Create a guide layer.

➤ Move a symbol around a guide.

➤ Rotate a symbol through 360°.

➤ Move and resize text symbols.

➤ Import sound files and add to layers.

➤ Add ActionScript commands to frames and buttons.

➤ Label frames.

➤ Create button symbols.

➤ Debug a file.

ASSESSMENT POINT

Now let's assess the work. Look back at the table at the beginning of this section (**Target point**) and decide on which of the statements you can answer 'Yes' to.

Did you do as well as you expected? Could you improve your work? Add a comment to your work to show what you could do to improve it so that next time you'll remember to do it the first time.

PRODUCING A SLIDESHOW

TASK BRIEF

The company really love your work. They love it so much that they are all coming up with ideas about how you can improve it. They have sent you the following email ...

From: Big Drinks Ltd

To: Design Studio

BRIEF

The Slurp can with the moving text and buttons is just what we need for the Internet advert. We would, however, like you to make more of a link with a healthy lifestyle and present some designs using digital photographs.

DESIGN STUDIO RESPONSE

 The digital images will show fruit and vegetables so people will associate them with the drink.

 The images will change from blurred to clear.

 There will be some animated text that tells the user about the drink.

There will be buttons so that the user can stop and start the animation.

As you work through the task you will find out why Design Studio made these choices.

SOFTWARE SKILLS

You will use the skills from Tasks 1 and 2 and learn how to:

> **Import** images to the Stage
> **Resize** the images to fit the Stage
> Convert the images to **movie clip** symbols
> Apply **blur filters** to the images.
> Add and animate **text**
> Create motion between the keyframes
> Add **command buttons** to allow the users to start and stop the slideshow

FUNCTIONAL SKILLS

As you work through this task the Functional Skills tabs will explain to you why the design company (Design Studio) responded to the brief from Big Drinks Ltd in the way they did and explain why they would choose to:

> Select certain images
> Search for images
> Edit images
> Recognise copyright

CAPABILITY

This time you have been asked to make decisions, so you will be demonstrating your capability through:

> Creating a presentation for a particular purpose
> Matching the presentation to an audience

These are the rules for creating an effective presentation.

VOCABULARY

You should learn some new words and understand what they mean.

> Movie clip
> Blur
> Audio
> Command button

RESOURCES

There are two files for this task that demonstrate what you will be creating in Flash:

Slurp3.fla

slurp3.swf

If you want to take a look at these files before you start you can download them from www.payne-gallway.co.uk

69

TARGET POINT

Have a look at the statements in this table before you start your task so you know what you are aiming for.

Although you will not be making your own decisions for much of this activity, these levels show you what you could be awarded when completing similar tasks on other work where you are working more independently and without following instructions.

Level 3	Level 4	Level 5	Level 6
You have searched for suitable images using a search with one keyword.	You have searched for suitable images using keywords such as 'fruit' and 'healthy'.	You have used keyword searches using three words together, e.g. 'fruit', 'health' and 'drink'.	You have completed an interactive presentation so that the user can control the animation.
You have added the images to the presentation.	You have selected suitable images.	You have selected suitable images from a large range.	You have checked that all of the code has been entered correctly.
You have saved the presentation with a suitable name.	You have used **Save As** to save the file with a new name – 'Slurp3'.	You have combined an image with text – the images of fruit and text to describe them.	
	You have saved the file in the correct folder.	You have added command buttons and tested them so that they work correctly.	
	You have positioned and resized the images.	You have put stop commands on to the timeline to stop the animation.	
	You have combined a suitable image and some text – you have added text to the images.	You have tested the buttons to ensure that they work.	
	You have added command buttons to control the animation.		

Before we get started:

So far we have used two types of symbols – graphic and button.

In this animation we are going to convert the images into **Movie Clip** symbols so that we can apply filters to them like a blurring effect.

Before you start any project, you should organise your area where you are going to save the work.

In the Flash folder, create another folder called **Task3** – this is where you will save the files you will be creating in this project.

OK. Let's get started.

We are going to create a new presentation, without the Slurp can this time.

We are going to use Flash to create a slideshow with animated text and command buttons to stop and start the action.

Before we start, we need to gather some assets that we will be using in the presentation. We need three pictures that show fruit and vegetables, and healthy fruit drinks. You should be able to search for some suitable images. The examples used in this book are shown here.

Fruit1   Fruit2   Fruit3

STEP 1: CREATING A NEW DOCUMENT AND ADDING LAYERS AND IMAGES

 Open Flash and create a new document.

Save it in the Task 3 folder as **Slurp3**.

> **IMPORTANT TIP**
> Remember: select Flash File (ActionScript 2.0).

Importing images to the Library

2 Change frame rate to 15 frames per second.

3 Import the three images to the Library.

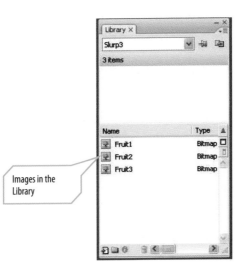

Images in the Library

Figure 3.1

4 Create three layers. Rename them **Fruit1**, **Fruit2** and **Fruit3**.

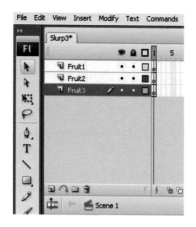

Figure 3.2

Locking layers

We are first going to work on the Fruit1 layer.

When you are working on one layer, you can easily change objects on other layers. But, because we don't want to do this, we will lock the layers we are not working on.

Click here to lock the layer. A padlock will appear showing that it is locked. Just click the padlock to unlock

Figure 3.3

STEP 2: ADDING THE FIRST FRUIT IMAGE AND ANIMATED TEXT

Now that Fruit2 and Fruit3 are locked, we can work on the Fruit1 layer.

Resizing images

 Drag the first picture to the Stage, which is currently showing frame 1 of the Fruit1 layer.

The Stage is 550 × 400 pixels.

If the picture is too large, we can easily resize it.

The easiest way is to use the **Properties** pane.

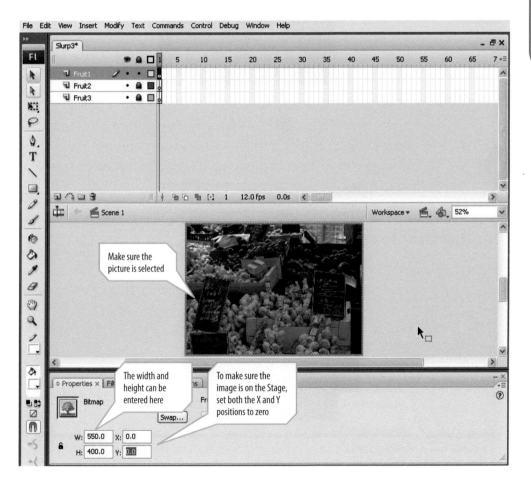

Figure 3.4

We want the picture to start off blurred and become clear over 45 frames – which is three seconds.

We will therefore need to convert it into a **Movie clip** symbol.

Creating Movie clip symbols

2 Select the picture and press **F8** to convert it into a **symbol**.

Name the symbol **Fruit1S** and Type as **Movie clip**.

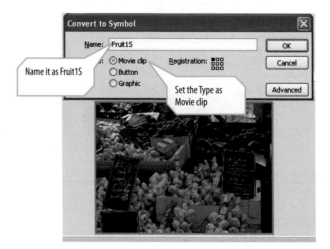

Figure 3.5

3 We have converted this image into a Movie clip symbol so that we can apply some effects to it.

Make sure the symbol on the Stage is selected and select the **Filters** tab on the Properties bar.

Figure 3.6

Using the Blur effect

 4 We can now apply some filters to this symbol.

Click on the **+** icon to see the options and select **Blur**.

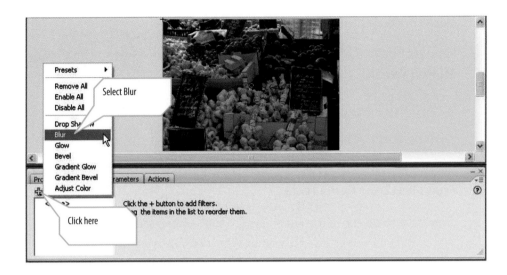

Figure 3.7

 5 Now change the Blur X and Blur Y boxes to **100%**.

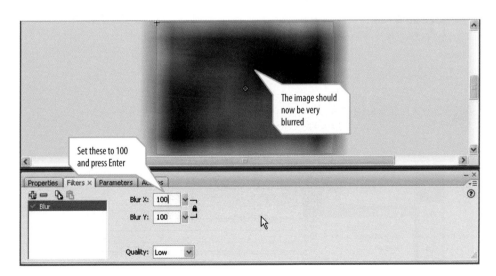

Figure 3.8

Later you can try out some of the other filters.

FUNCTIONAL SKILLS

Altering images – we have chosen to add an effect to the image, to add suspense to the advert and make people want to watch it to find out what happens

Insert a keyframe at frame 45 of the Fruit1 layer.

 Select the blurred image on this frame and change the Blur X and Blur Y factors back to **0** so that the image is now clear.

This now means that between frames 1 and 45, the image will gradually become clearer once we have created motion tween.

 Right click on one of the frames between frames 1 and 45 and select **Create Motion Tween**.

Now press Ctrl-Enter to test it.

Yes, it gradually changes from blurred to clear over three seconds. Excellent!

 Now add three layers above the Fruit1 layer and rename them as **Fruit1Text1**, **Fruit1Text2** and **Fruit1Text3**.

They have to be above the Fruit1 layer so that we can see them.

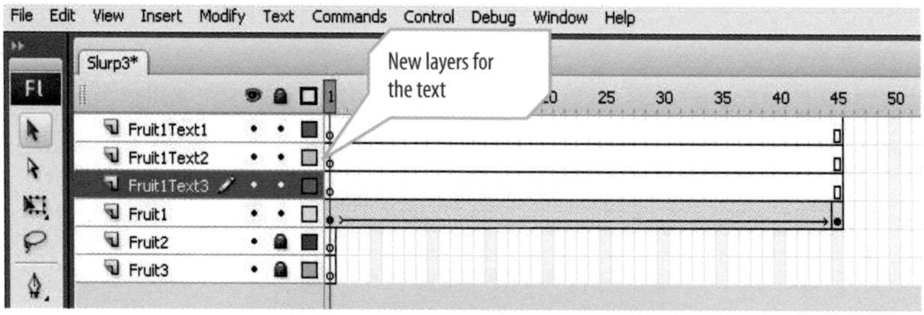

Figure 3.9

10 For each of these three layers insert a keyframe at frame 45.

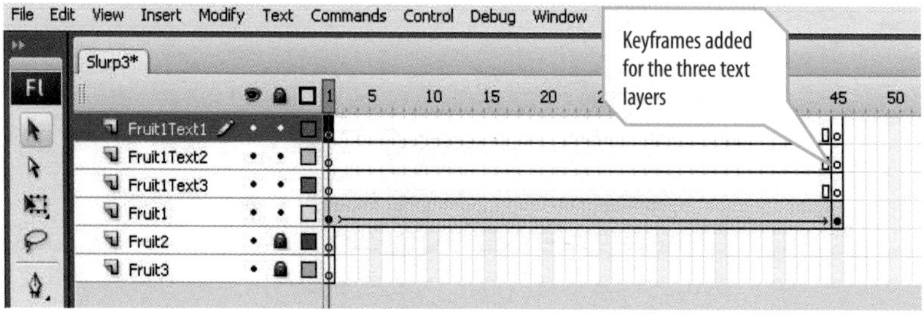

Figure 3.10

11 Select **frame 45** of the **Fruit1Text1** layer and use the **Text Tool** to enter the following text: **Fruit**.

Figure 3.11

The font size in this example is 60 and it is bold.

Animating text

12 Use the **Selection Tool** to select the text and press **F8** to convert it into a symbol.

Name it as **Text1** and make it a **Graphic** symbol.

Figure 3.12

13 Now select **frame 45** of the **Fruit1Text2** layer and use the Text Tool to enter the following text: **for**.

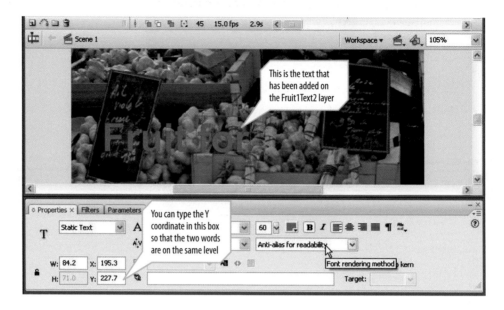

Figure 3.13

14 Use the **Selection Tool** to select the text and press **F8** to convert it into a symbol.

Name it as **Text2** and make it a **Graphic** symbol.

15 Now select **frame 45** of the **Fruit1Text3** layer and use the Text Tool to enter the following text: 'SLURP'.

Figure 3.14

16 Use the **Selection Tool** to select the text and press **F8** to convert it into a symbol.

Name it as **Text3** and make it a **Graphic** symbol.

We now have three new layers with a graphic symbol on each layer.

At frame 45, they are all lined up to read **Fruit for SLURP**.

We now have to move them to their starting positions in frame 1 so that over the 45 frames they will move to their final positions.

Select the Fruit1Text1 layer and click on frame 1.

Drag the **Text1** symbol from the Library and place it in the top right-hand corner of the Stage.

Figure 3.15

Insert a keyframe at frame 15 in the Fruit1Text1 layer and move the Text1 symbol to a new position at the left, as shown in Figure 3.16.

Figure 3.16

19 Insert a keyframe at frame 30 and move the symbol again, as shown in Figure 3.17.

Figure 3.17

20 Right click on the Fruit1Text1 layer between frames 1 and 15 and click on **Create Motion Tween**.

21 Do the same between all the keyframes so that the arrows appear between the keyframes.

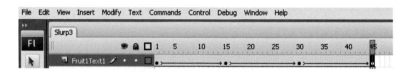

Figure 3.18

22 Save the file (Slurp3) and then press Ctrl-Enter to test it.

The word 'Fruit' should move across the screen and finish in its final position as the image changes from blurred to clear.

23 We now have to do the same for the Fruit1Text2 and Fruit1Text3 layers to move the words 'for' and 'SLURP'.

This can be done in the same way. Use these instructions to help you:

❯ Select the layer (Fruit1Text2 or Fruit1Text3).

❯ Select frame 1 of the layer.

❯ Drag in the symbol from the Library (Text2 or Text3).

❯ Position it where you want it to start.

❯ **Insert Keyframes** at frames 15 and 30.

➤ Move the symbols where you want them to be on those frames.

➤ **Create Motion Tween** the keyframes.

Go on, press Ctrl-Enter and try it out.

Yes, that works – but it would be good for the reader to see the finished animation for a second before it moves on. We can easily do that.

 Right click on the Fruit1 timeline at frame 60 and select **Insert Frame**. This will copy frame 45 onto all the frames up to frame 60.

Do the same for the Fruit1Text1, Fruit1Text2 and Fruit1Text3 layers.

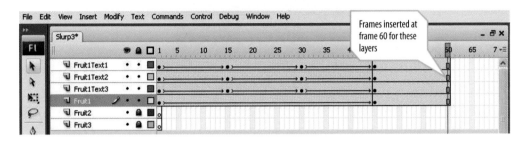

Figure 3.19

STEP 3: ADDING THE SECOND FRUIT IMAGE AND ANIMATED TEXT

 You can now **unlock** the **Fruit2 layer** and lock all of the others.

 Insert a keyframe at frame 61 of the Fruit2 layer.

 Drag in the Fruit2 picture. (Make sure it is unlocked!)

> **IMPORTANT TIP**
> You did all of this for the Fruit1 layer.

 Change the size to 550 × 400 pixels and position it on the Stage by changing the X and Y coordinates both to 0.

 Select the picture and convert it to a **Movie clip** symbol called **Fruit2S**.

 Add the **Blur filter** and change the X and Y settings to 100.

 Insert a keyframe on the Fruit2 layer at frame 105.

 Select the symbol on the Stage and change the Blur settings on this frame to 0.

 Right click between the keyframes and **Create Motion Tween**.

2 Create a new layer and rename it as **Fruit2Text**.

❯ Drag the layer so that is just above the Fruit2 layer.

❯ Insert a keyframe at frame **105** of this Fruit2Text layer.

❯ Use the **Text Tool** to write 'Fresh and Healthy' at the bottom of the picture as shown in Figure 3.20.

Figure 3.20

❯ Select the text and convert it to a graphic symbol called **Fruit2Text**.

❯ Insert a keyframe at frame 61 and drag in the Fruit2Text symbol.

❯ Use the **Free Transform Tool** to resize it and to turn it upside down. Position it near the top of the picture.

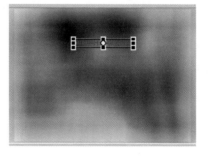

Figure 3.21

Now insert a keyframe at frame 75. Move, resize and turn the text symbol.

Figure 3.22

 Insert a keyframe at frame 90 and again move, resize and turn the text.

Figure 3.23

 Now **Create Motion Tween** keyframes 61, 75, 90 and 105.

As we want the user to be able to look at the finished slide for a second, **Insert Frame** at frame 120 of the Fruit2 and Fruit2Text layers.

The timeline should be like that shown in Figure 3.24.

Figure 3.24

STEP 4: ADDING THE THIRD FRUIT IMAGE AND ANIMATED TEXT

 You can now **unlock** the **Fruit3 layer** and lock all of the others.

 Insert a keyframe at frame 121 of the Fruit3 layer.

Drag in the Fruit3 picture. (Make sure it is unlocked!)

Change the size to 550 × 400 pixels and position it on the Stage by setting the X and Y coordinates to 0.

Select the picture and convert it to a **Movie clip** symbol called **Fruit3S**.

Add the **Blur filter** and change the X and Y settings to 100.

Insert a keyframe on the Fruit3 layer at frame 165.

Select the symbol on the Stage and change the Blur settings on this frame to 0.

Right click between the keyframes and **Create Motion Tween**.

 Create a new layer and rename it as **Fruit3Text**.

Drag it so that it is immediately above the Fruit3 layer.

Insert a keyframe at frame 121 of this layer and use the Text Tool to add the following text in the top of the picture: 'Drink the Fruit'.

Convert it to a graphic symbol called **Fruit3Text**.

Figure 3.25

This time we are going to change the colour of the text over the frames.

Changing symbol colours

3 To change the colour, select the Fruit3Text symbol and select **Advanced** from the **Color** list in the **Properties** pane.

Figure 3.26

4 Select the **Settings** button.

Figure 3.27

5 You can now use the sliders to change the colour by changing the red, green and blue settings.

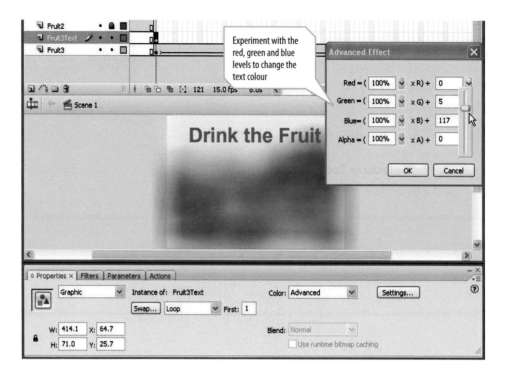

Figure 3.28

6 When you are happy with the starting colour, **Insert Keyframes** every five frames up to frame 165 and change the colour on each.

Now **Create Motion Tween** these keyframes.

Insert Frame at frame 180 for both the Fruit3 and Fruit3Text layers.

Figure 3.29

Don't forget to save the Flash file again.

Now go on – try it out again!

STEP 5: ADDING COMMAND BUTTONS

All we have to do now is to add the command buttons. We did some in Task 2, so it should be pretty easy!

 Create two new layers. Rename them as **OnButton** and **OffButton**.

Drag them to the top of the stack with the OnButton first.

> **TIP**
> It may be useful to lock all of the other layers when you follow this step.

 On frame 1 of the OnButton layer, create a button like the one below.

Use the **Selection Tool** to select both the circle and text and press **F8** to convert into a Button symbol called OnButton.

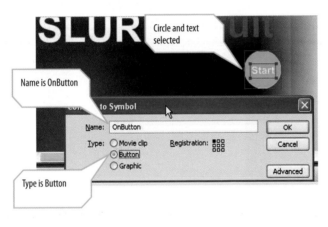

Figure 3.30

 Select the symbol and open the **Actions** pane.

Enter the following, exactly as it appears:

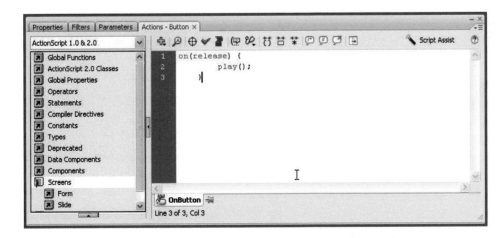

Figure 3.31

That is:

```
on(release) {
play();
}
```

4 Select the **Properties** tab to close the **Actions** pane.

5 On frame 1 of the OffButton layer, create an off button.

Convert it into a button symbol called **OffButton**.

Open the **Actions** pane and enter the following text exactly as it appears in Figure 3.32:

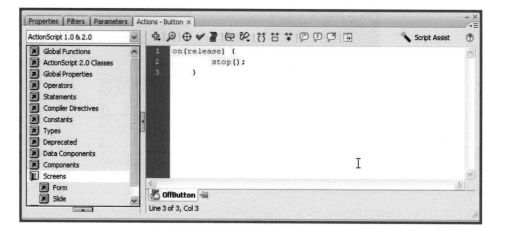

Figure 3.32

That is:

```
on(release) {
stop();
}
```

6 Select the Properties tab to close the Actions pane.

ALL DONE

Try it out again. Check that the animations work as expected and that the buttons start and stop the animation.

Congratulations! You have just completed Task 3!

Now let's assess the work. Check which of the following you have completed.

CHECKPOINT

You should be able to:

- ❯ Import images to the Library.
- ❯ Lock layers.
- ❯ Resize images and centre them on the Stage.
- ❯ Convert images to Movie clip symbols.
- ❯ Blur images.
- ❯ Animate and rotate text.
- ❯ Change text symbol colours.
- ❯ Add and program command buttons.

ASSESSMENT POINT

Now let's assess the work. Look back at the table at the beginning of this section (**Target point**) and decide on which of the statements you can answer 'Yes' to.

Did you do as well as you expected? Could you improve your work? Add a comment to your work to show what you could do to improve it so that next time you'll remember to do it the first time.

TASK BRIEF

The Sandon Leisure Centre is launching a 'keep fit and healthy' promotion aimed at younger people. They have sent an email to all the local schools about a competition for students.

PROJECT BRIEF

From: The Sandon Leisure Centre
To: Schools

Project title: Competition for students

Background information: As part of our 'Keep Fit and Healthy' promotion, The Sandon Leisure Centre is opening a new café serving only healthy food and drinks. We want students to produce an interactive advert for the new café featuring the sorts of food and drinks that will be available.

Big Drinks Ltd are sponsoring the new café and Slurp will be one of the healthy drinks served.

Project outline: The new café will be advertised on the Internet and the leisure centre requires a Flash movie that can be used on their website.

PROJECT REQUIREMENTS

 The movie should last for 10 seconds with a frame rate of 15 frames per second.

 It should contain images, text and sound.

 The advert should contain at least three images and **two buttons** to allow the user to interact with the movie.

 The advert should be colourful and energetic.

Key message: The new café will be attractive to young people and will feature a range of exciting, healthy food and drinks.

Level 3	Level 4	Level 5	Level 6
You have searched for images using a single keyword, e.g. 'fruit'	You have made a plan of how you are going to solve the problem – to produce an advert	You have made a plan of how you will produce the advert and it shows in detail how it will advertise the drink	You have made a detailed plan and have shown how it will appeal to the target audience, 14–18-year-olds
You have collected three suitable images	You have used keyword searches using two words to search for suitable images, e.g. 'food' and 'healthy'	You have used keyword searches using three words together, e.g. 'fruit', 'health' and 'drink'	You have used complex keyword searches and have navigated to the correct parts of the websites to locate the information
You have saved your Flash file in a suitable folder	You have selected appropriate images and sounds from your searches	You have selected appropriate images from a large selection and they are appropriate for the audience	You have selected appropriate images from a large selection and you have asked users if they are appropriate for the audience and have considered the copyright issues
You have included text and images in your presentation	You have used **Save As** to save the file with a new name	You have combined text, images and sound, and have edited them to make sure they are appropriate to the audience	You have edited the images and sound so that they fit perfectly into the animation to make it suitable for the audience and purpose
You have produced a presentation that advertises the drink including images and text	You have saved the file in the correct folder	You have added command buttons and have programmed them to start and stop the animation	
	You have combined text, images and sound in a presentation	You have written instructions to make the command buttons start and stop the animation	
	You have presented information in the Flash movie including text and images	You have presented information in the Flash movie, including text and images, and it is suitable for the audience	
	You have moved and positioned the images and have chosen suitable fonts	You have edited the images and text to ensure it is suitable for the audience	
	Some of the information you have selected is suitable for the audience	All of the information you have selected is suitable for the audience	
	You have checked that the animation runs correctly	You have also checked that the command buttons work correctly	

⊕ TARGET POINT

Have a look at the following statements before you start your project so you know what you are aiming for.

Your task now is to create this Flash movie.

You have all of the skills you'll need to build the movie. Now you have to demonstrate your capability and produce an advert with a particular purpose and audience in mind.

Creating a presentation for a particular purpose (e.g. to advertise a drink) and for a particular audience (e.g. people between 9 and 14) is a big job, but the following steps will help you to work through it. You are going to concentrate on Steps 3, 4 and 5 in this project.

> **Step 1:** Identify the audience and purpose.

> **Step 2:** Analyse the audience needs and your idea.

> **Step 3:** Design and plan your solution.

> **Step 4:** Implement (create) your design.

> **Step 5:** Test your solution.

> **Step 6:** Evaluate your solution.

Before we get started – let's think.

For this project you will need to:

 Design the screens:

> The images you will you use.

> The text you will you need.

> Colour schemes.

> The audio for the advert.

 Plan the motion:

> How will the different images move from one to the other?

> How will the text move and change?

> How will you use buttons to control the movement?

> When will the audio change from one sound to another?

3 Collect all of the assets:

> Search for and collect all of the images you could use.

> Collect, create and edit the audio you will need.

4 Create your advert.

 Test your advert:

> Check that it lasts for 10 seconds.

> Check that all of the images and text move correctly.

> Check that the buttons work.

> Get feedback from people who the advert is aimed at.

To meet this project brief you need to complete Step 4, but that is only one part of the process that you would need to go through if you were designing this advert for a real leisure centre. The information below shows you how you could go about tackling the other steps in the process. Use the target points to decide how and which of the other steps you want to tackle. The Functional Skills tabs show you the skills you will be demonstrating in your work but remember you have to be able to say *why* you have chosen to use them in a particular way.

OK. Let's get started.

PLANNING THE MOVIE

All projects need to be planned for several reasons:

> They show your ideas all together so you can easily present them to your client – and they are easy and cheap to change if your client doesn't like them

> When the project is under way, you can keep looking back at the documents to make sure you have done everything you needed to

 You will first have to decide on the images you are going to use in the advert:

> How many?

> What will the images show?

> Where will I get the images from – will I create them myself, scan the pictures, take digital photographs or search for them on the Internet?

In your word-processing software, create a table that lists the images you are going to use like the one below:

What the image will show	Source of the image
The Slurp can	I will create this in Flash
Picture of young people with fruit drink	I will take a digital photograph
Picture of café with fruit	I will find a picture on the Internet

 You will have to decide on the sounds that you are going to use:

> Where will I get the sounds from – will I record them myself, rip them from a CD or find them on the Internet?

> Will they need editing?

> How will I edit them?

In your word-processing software, create a table like the one above to list the audio files you will be using.

C You can now produce storyboards for the screens. You could draw these yourself or create them in word-processing or presentation software. **Storyboards** are just a series of drawings displayed in sequence so that you can imagine what an animation might look like. There is an example below of one that Big Drinks Ltd created for their interactive advert for Slurp. You will need to draw several storyboards – one for each of the main screens.

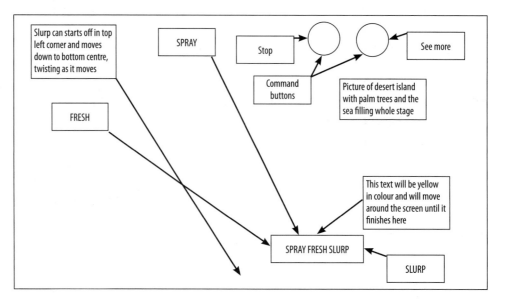

Figure Project.1

D You will now have to plan out the movement and timings of the images. You could draw a timeline showing the 150 frames and show where the screens will appear and change. There is an example below of one that Big Drinks Ltd created for their interactive advert for Slurp. The top row shows the frame number (up to frame 50) and the bottom boxes show the scenes and what is happening in each one. You can see that each scene lasts for two seconds.

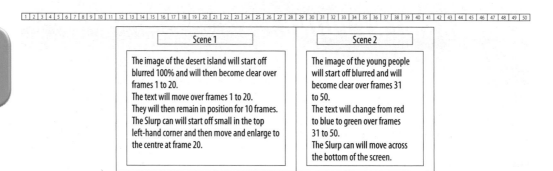

Figure Project.2

E You can now draw a table listing all of the assets you will be using, where you have got them from and how you have edited them. Here is an example.

Asset	Source	How edited	Where used
Slurp can	I drew this myself in Flash	Resized and rotated where necessary	Used in scene 2 (frames 31 to 50) and in scene 4 (frames 100 to 150)
Music file 1	On the Internet from a royalty-free site	Edited in Audacity so that it lasted for two seconds	Used in scene 1 (frames 1 to 30)

FUNCTIONAL SKILLS
Adding and altering suitable tables

When you have got a working design, you can start to create the movie. If you change the plan you will have to list the changes you have made. When you have finished the advert, don't forget to save it and publish it.

 All that remains to be done is to test it. You could create a table in your word-processing software to show the tests you have carried out. Use the project brief and the **Target point** statements to help you identify what your tests should be. Below is an example.

Test	Comment
The movie lasts for 10 seconds	
I have used at least three images	
The images change as in the plan	
The text moves and changes	
The sound files play at the correct times	
The stop button works correctly	
The start button works correctly	
The advert is suitable for 14–18-year-olds	
The advert shows that the drink is 'healthy'	
The advert shows that the drink is 'cool'	

ASSESSMENT POINT

All that you need to do now is to get some feedback from some test users in your group. Ask them to comment on the images, sounds and text you have used, whether it is suitable for 14–18-year-olds, and if they think it shows that the café is cool and that it will feature healthy food and drinks. You could write up their comments using your word-processing software.

You should assess your own work too. Look back at the table at the beginning of this section (**Target point**) and decide on which of the statements you can answer 'Yes' to.

Did you do as well as you expected? Could you improve your work? Add a comment to your work to show what you could do to improve it so that next time you'll remember to do it the first time.

FUNCTIONAL SKILLS
Review and modify documents to help you next time

INDEX